Spellcaster Publishing

Soft Paws and a Little Tail

© 2018 H.L.C.

All rights reserved. No part of this document may be reproduced or transmitted in any form or by any means, electronic, mechanical, photocopying, recording, or otherwise, without prior written permission of H.L.C.

First Printing: 2018

ISBN-13: 978-1732225404
ISBN-10: 1732225400

All artwork, wording, and design features of this book by H.L.C.
For more information, contact spellcaster.leafblaze@gmail.com

This book belongs to
_____
and was written by
_____

 My Mommy and Daddy

My Mommy's name is
_____

Everyone calls her _____

Her birthday is _____

She was born (location, date, etc.)
_____

She has many talents _____
_____

My favorite thing to do with her is _____

My Mommy

My Daddy's name is
_____

Everyone calls him _____

His birthday is _____

He was born (location, date, etc.)
_____

He has many talents _____
_____

My favorite thing to do with him is _____

My Daddy

I have other relatives too!
Here's the rest of my family …

Names and birthdates of my relatives

Brothers _____ _____ _____ _____

Sisters _____ _____ _____ _____

Maternal grandparents _____ _____

Paternal grandparents _____ _____

Aunts _____ _____ _____ _____

Uncles _____ _____ _____ _____

Cousins _____ _____ _____ _____

Other _____ _____ _____ _____
_____ _____ _____ _____

Pictures of my family

I also have a great human family...

Names and birthdates of my human family

Mom and Dad _____ _____

Brothers _____ _____ _____ _____

Sisters _____ _____ _____ _____

Maternal grandparents _____ _____

Paternal grandparents _____ _____

Aunts _____ _____ _____ _____

Uncles _____ _____ _____ _____

Cousins _____ _____ _____ _____

Other _____ _____ _____ _____
_____ _____ _____ _____

Pictures of my human family

We're getting a kitten!

The day my family discovered that my mommy was pregnant/ I was being adopted _____
_____
The first ones who knew were _____
Everyone was so excited! When they heard about it, they _____
_____
They celebrated by _____
My due date/ arrival date was _____
The name of my vet/breeder/shelter was _____

Mommy when she was expecting/ my shelter

A special party was held for Mommy, Daddy, and me to celebrate my coming arrival…

Host/Hostess _____ Date _____
Location _____
Guests _____   Gifts _____

Invitations and Pictures of the Party

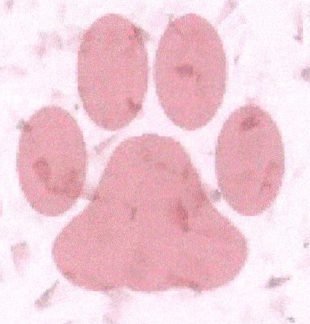

My mommy was growing . . .

 . . . and so was my family's excitement!

Pictures of my waiting family

There were many useful books and lessons that my family used to prepare for me _____
_____

They also bought toys, a bed, and lots of other stuff to get ready for me
_____
_____

Here I come ...

I was born at/adopted from _____
and was delivered by _____
Mommy's reaction was _____
_____
Daddy's reaction was _____
_____
The other people who were there when I arrived were _____
_____
Everyone else reacted by _____
_____

My first picture

XoXoXoXoXoXoXoXoXoXo
Here I am!

A picture of little me

My name is _____, which was chosen for me because _____
I arrived at _____ on _____
I weigh _____ and am _____ long
My eyes are _____ and my fur is _____
I look the most like _____

xOxOxOxOxOxOxOxOxOx

My birth/adoption certificate

My first day home!

Me at home

On my first day at home, the date was _____ and the weather was _____
My new address was _____
I had a special spot just for me that _____
_____
Things were pretty busy at first ... _____
_____
_____

Homecoming Fun

People who visited me . . .

_____
_____
_____
_____
_____
_____
_____
_____
_____
_____
_____
_____
_____

Gifts and cards . . .

_____
_____
_____
_____
_____
_____
_____
_____
_____
_____
_____
_____
_____

When I was born/adopted...

Current events: _____
_____

Headlines in local news: _____
_____

National news: _____
_____

World news: _____
_____

World leaders: _____
_____

Sports heroes: _____
_____

Popular songs and musicians: _____
_____

The leader of our country: _____
_____

Best-selling books: _____
_____
Popular movies and actors: _____
_____
Popular television shows: _____
_____
Internet fads: _____
_____
Popular websites: _____
_____
Fashion trends: _____
_____
Favorite pastimes of my family: _____
_____
_____
_____

Common Costs

A house _____ Gas _____
A movie ticket _____ Litter _____ A car _____
A computer _____ A smartphone _____ Milk _____
A leash _____ Cat food _____ Dog food _____

Vet Visits

My vet _____ Phone number _____
Office address _____
On my first visit _____
_____

Visits:

Date	Purpose	Treatment	Notes
_____	_____	_____	_____
_____	_____	_____	_____
_____	_____	_____	_____
_____	_____	_____	_____
_____	_____	_____	_____
_____	_____	_____	_____
_____	_____	_____	_____
_____	_____	_____	_____
_____	_____	_____	_____
_____	_____	_____	_____
_____	_____	_____	_____
_____	_____	_____	_____

Immunizations

	Date	Reaction
Rabies	_____	_____
Panleukopenia (Feline distemper)	_____	_____
Feline Viral Respiratory Disease Complex	_____	_____
Feline Leukemia	_____	_____

_____ _____ _____
_____ _____ _____
_____ _____ _____
_____ _____ _____

Me getting ready for the vet

play • pounce • swat • nap • chase
I'm growing up!

Date	Age	Length	Height	Weight

mew • climb • jump • purr • cuddle

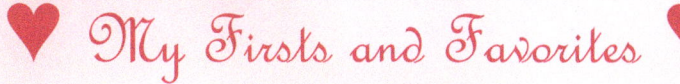
♥ My Firsts and Favorites ♥

The first time I …
Rode in a car/plane/train/boat _____
_____
_____
Learned a trick _____
_____
Slept the whole night _____
_____
Ate solid food _____
_____
Other firsts _____
_____
_____
_____
_____
_____
_____
_____
_____
_____
_____

Every day I _____
_____
_____
I loved to eat _____
_____
I didn't like eating _____
_____
My favorite toys _____
_____
My best friends _____
_____
Getting groomed was _____
_____
Car rides were _____
_____
Other favorites _____
_____
_____
_____
_____
_____
_____
_____

*Pictures of me as
I learn and grow . . .*

XO Holidays and Celebrations XO

My family celebrates _____
_____

My first time celebrating _____ was on
_____ and we celebrated it by _____
_____

My first time celebrating _____ was on
_____ and we celebrated it by _____
_____

My first time celebrating _____ was on
_____ and we celebrated it by _____
_____

My first time celebrating _____ was on
_____ and we celebrated it by _____
_____

My first time celebrating _____ was on
_____ and we celebrated it by _____
_____

Some other family traditions are _____
_____
_____

Family and friends present _____
_____
_____

xOxOxOxOxOxOxOx

Xo *Pictures of the festivities* Xo
... and me!

xOxOxOxOxOxOxOx

My First Birthday!

We celebrated by _____
_____

Family and friends there _____
_____

Gifts I received _____
_____

Pictures of me on
my birthday

*Invitation and
pictures of the party*

 # My Second Birthday

Birthday Pictures

_____
_____
_____
_____
_____
_____
_____
_____
_____
_____

 *My Third Birthday*

Birthday Pictures

_____
_____
_____
_____
_____
_____
_____
_____
_____
_____

 # My Fourth Birthday

Birthday Pictures

 # My Fifth Birthday

Birthday Pictures

_____
_____
_____
_____
_____
_____
_____
_____
_____

Notes, Photos, Keepsakes, etc.

Notes, Photos, Keepsakes, etc.

XoXoXoXoXoXoXoXoXo
Notes, Photos, Keepsakes, etc.

xOxOxOxOxOxOxOxOx

XoXoXoXoXoXoXoXo
Notes, Photos, Keepsakes, etc.

xOxOxOxOxOxOxOx

Authored and Illustrated by H.L.C.

In addition to her human family, Hannah has a menagerie of pets who have spent more than twelve years overseeing her training as a pet "owner." Both families were instrumental in assisting her with the writing, editing, and illustrating of her books. When not studying for college exams, she enjoys reading, gardening, cooking, and taking pictures of furry friends and food.

www.ingramcontent.com/pod-product-compliance
Lightning Source LLC
Chambersburg PA
CBHW041819040426
42452CB00004B/155